Microwave
SOUPS AND APPETIZERS

Text by Judith Ferguson
Photography by Peter Barry
Designed by Philip Clucas

© 1987 Illustrations and text: Colour Library Books Ltd.,
    Guildford, Surrey, England.
Text filmsetting by Focus Photoset Ltd., London, England.
All rights reserved.
Printed and bound in Barcelona, Spain by Cronión, S.A.
1987 edition published by Crescent Books, distributed by Crown Publishers, Inc.
ISBN 0 517 640783
h g f e d c b a

Microwave
SOUPS AND APPETIZERS

CRESCENT BOOKS
NEW YORK

4

Contents

INTRODUCTION

Soups and appetizers are the beginnings of a great meal. To make a memorable start, carefully consider how the soup or appetizer will co-ordinate with the rest of the meal. Consider color, texture and variety of ingredients.

Are soups and appetizers reserved only for the beginning of a meal? Absolutely not. They can be meals in themselves: soups, accompanied by salads and good bread, make wonderful cold weather lunches and dinners, while appetizers can double as light meals anytime. Microwave cooking makes light work of a light meal.

Soups can easily be made in small quantities in a microwave oven. Depending on your oven and your own preference, you may want to add 1½ times the flour quantity when adapting soup recipes for microwave cooking. Liquids do not evaporate as fast in microwave cooking as they do in conventional cooking and so more thickening may be required. The soup recipes in this book have been designed to include standing time, but always allow 1 to 2 minutes when adapting any soup recipe for your microwave oven.

Sauce recipes may need more flour, too, depending on your oven. These recipes were tested in a 700 watt maximum oven, but ovens with a lower maximum wattage may require a recipe with more flour.

Soufflés wait for no one, and those made in a microwave oven are no exception. I've included one, though, because they cook in a matter of minutes and are great fun to watch. Beware of over-cooking, though.

Pâtés are one food the microwave oven cooks excellently, and in a fraction of the time taken in a conventional oven. A custard cup of water in the oven with the pâté or terrine keeps the mixture moist.

A microwave oven can be a great boon when giving a dinner party. Preparations can be made ahead of time and then your first course can be reheated in a matter of minutes while you relax with your guests. Better still, soups and starters can be cooked and reheated in their serving dishes, providing they are safe for the microwave oven. Think of the advantage that will give when the time comes to washing the dishes!

Microwave
SOUPS AND APPETIZERS

CREAM AND PURÉE SOUPS

Crab Bisque

PREPARATION TIME: 15 minutes

MICROWAVE COOKING TIME:
17 minutes

SERVES: 4 people

SOUP
1lb crabmeat, fresh or frozen
3 tbsps butter or margarine
3 tbsps flour
1 shallot finely chopped
2 cups milk
½ cup cream
1 cup fish or chicken stock
1 bay leaf
Salt
Pepper
Tabasco
2 tbsps dry sherry

CROÛTONS
2 tbsps butter or margarine
2 slices bread, crusts removed
Salt
Pepper
Paprika

Put butter and shallot into a casserole. Cover and cook for 3 minutes on HIGH, stirring occasionally. Stir in the flour and cook for 2 minutes on HIGH. Stir in the milk, stock, seasonings, bay leaf and a few drops of tabasco and cover and cook on HIGH for 5 minutes, stirring frequently. Blend in the crabmeat and sherry. Cook on MEDIUM for 3-4 minutes. To prepare croûtons, place butter in a small bowl and cook on LOW for 15-20 seconds or until softened. Cut each slice of bread into 12-16 squares, depending on the size and thickness of the slices. Toss the cubes of bread in the melted butter with salt and pepper. Spread the bread out on a flat plate. Sprinkle the bread with paprika and cook on HIGH for 1½-2 minutes or until the croûtons are firm but not crisp. Stir and turn the croûtons several times during

This page: Crab Bisque (top) and Cream of Chicken Soup (bottom). Facing page: Cream of Cucumber Soup (top) and Leek and Potato Soup (bottom).

cooking. Let them stand for 5 minutes before serving. Re-heat the soup on HIGH for 1 minute. Stir in the cream just before serving, top with the croûtons and dust with more paprika.

Leek and Potato Soup

PREPARATION TIME: 10 minutes

MICROWAVE COOKING TIME: 20 minutes

SERVES: 4 people

3 leeks, washed and sliced thinly
3½ cups potatoes, diced
3 tbsps butter or margarine
2 cups milk
1½ cups chicken or vegetable stock
1 bay leaf
¼ tsp thyme
Salt
Pepper

GARNISH
1 bunch chives, chopped
½ cup sour cream

Put leeks, potatoes and butter into a large bowl. Cover with plastic wrap and pierce several times. Cook on HIGH for 10 minutes. Add milk, stock, thyme, bay leaf and seasoning, and cook for 7 minutes on HIGH. Leave standing, covered, for 1 minute. Uncover and allow to cool slightly. Remove bay leaf, pour soup into a food processor, and purée until smooth. Check seasoning and heat through for 3 minutes on HIGH. Serve with a spoonful of sour cream and chopped chives for each individual portion.

Cream of Chicken Soup

PREPARATION TIME: 15 minutes

MICROWAVE COOKING TIME: 31 minutes

SERVES: 4 people

1lb chicken breasts
1½ cups water
2 cups milk

1 chicken bouillon cube
2 tbsps butter
2 tbsps flour
¼ cup heavy cream
1 bay leaf
1 sprig thyme
¼ tsp sage, fresh or dried
Salt
Pepper

GARNISH
1 bunch chives, chopped

Put the chicken into a large bowl with the water. Cover with plastic wrap, pierce several times, and cook for 15 minutes on HIGH. Remove chicken from bowl and leave to cool. Strain the liquid from the chicken and set it aside. Put butter and flour into the bowl and cook for 1 minute on HIGH. Gradually stir in the liquid from the chicken and the milk. Add bay leaf, thyme and seasoning, and cook for 4 minutes on HIGH, stirring occasionally. Remove skin and bone from chicken, and cut into small pieces. Crumble the bouillon cube and add to the bowl along with the chicken and sage. Cook, uncovered, for 10 minutes on HIGH. Add cream and cook for 1 minute on HIGH. Serve garnished with chopped chives.

Lentil Soup with Smoked Sausage

PREPARATION TIME: 10 minutes

MICROWAVE COOKING TIME: 60-70 minutes

SERVES: 4 people

½lb smoked sausage
1½ cups brown lentils, washed
1 medium onion, chopped
1 bay leaf
¼ tsp thyme
1 tbsp Worcester sauce
Powdered cloves
4 cups chicken or vegetable stock

GARNISH
⅓ cup Parmesan cheese, grated

Put onion into a large bowl. Cover with plastic wrap and pierce in

several places. Cook for 8 minutes on HIGH, or until onion is softened. Add lentils, herbs, Worcester sauce, pinch of powdered cloves and the stock. Re-cover bowl and cook on HIGH for about 20 minutes, stirring well. Reduce setting to MEDIUM and cook for about 20 minutes, stirring well. Remove skin from smoked sausage if desired. Add sausage to the bowl, and continue to cook for another 20-30 minutes, or until lentils are soft. Remove the bay leaf and the sausage. Purée the soup if desired. Slice the sausage into thin rounds and add to the soup. Stir soup well and adjust seasoning. Serve garnished with Parmesan cheese.

Creamy Spinach Soup

PREPARATION TIME: 15 minutes

MICROWAVE COOKING TIME: 16 minutes

SERVES: 4 people

2lbs fresh spinach, washed and stems
    removed
2 tbsps butter or margarine
2 tbsps flour
1 shallot, finely chopped
1½ cups milk
1½ cups chicken or vegetable stock
½ cup cream
¼ tsp marjoram
Squeeze of lemon juice
Grated nutmeg
Salt
Pepper

GARNISH
1 hard-boiled egg, chopped

Put washed spinach into a roasting bag and tie loosely. Stand the bag upright in the oven and cook for 2 minutes on HIGH, or until spinach has wilted. (It can also be cooked in a bowl covered with pierced plastic

Facing page: Creamy Spinach Soup (top) and Lentil Soup with Smoked Sausage (bottom).

wrap.) Put shallot and butter into a large bowl, cover and cook for 5 minutes on HIGH. Add flour, and cook for 2 minutes on HIGH. Stir in the milk and stock, and add marjoram, bay leaf and grated nutmeg. Cook for 2 minutes on HIGH, stirring occasionally. Add spinach, salt, pepper and lemon juice, and cook for 3 minutes on HIGH. Pour soup into a food processor and purée until smooth. Add cream, and adjust seasoning. Heat through for 2 minutes on HIGH. Serve garnished with egg.

Bouillabaisse

PREPARATION TIME: 15 minutes

MICROWAVE COOKING TIME: 10 minutes

SERVES: 4 people

1lb assorted fish (eg monkfish, red snapper, cod, white fish, rock salmon)
½lb assorted cooked shellfish (shrimp, lobster, crab)
2 leeks, cleaned and thinly sliced
1 small bulb Florentine fennel, sliced
2 tbsps olive oil
4 tomatoes, skinned, seeded and roughly chopped
1 tbsp tomato paste
3 cups water
⅔ cup white wine
1 clove garlic, crushed
1 strip orange rind
½ tsp saffron
1 bay leaf
1 tsp lemon juice
1 tbsp chopped parsley
Salt
Pepper

GARNISH
4 slices French bread, toasted
¼ cup prepared mayonnaise, mixed with 1 clove garlic, crushed, and a pinch of Cayenne pepper

Cut fish into 2″ pieces. Remove shells from shellfish and cut crab and lobster into small pieces. Put leeks, fennel, garlic and olive oil into a large casserole. Cover and cook for 3 minutes on HIGH. Add orange

rind, saffron, bay leaf, lemon juice, water and wine. Stir in the tomato paste and seasoning, and mix well. Add fish and tomatoes and cook for 5 minutes, covered, on HIGH. Add shellfish and parsley, and cook for 2 minutes on HIGH. Mix the mayonnaise, garlic and Cayenne pepper and spread on the pieces of toasted French bread. Place bread in the bottom of the serving dish and spoon over the soup.

Cream of Celery Soup

PREPARATION TIME: 10 minutes

MICROWAVE COOKING TIME: 32 minutes

SERVES: 4 people

4 cups chopped celery, leaves reserved
1 shallot, finely chopped
2 tbsps butter
2 tbsps flour
1 cup chicken or vegetable stock
1½ cups milk
½ cup heavy cream
1 tbsp celery seeds (optional)
1 bay leaf
1 sprig thyme
Salt
Pepper

Put butter into a large casserole and heat for 1 minute on HIGH. Add celery and shallot, then cover and

**This page: Bouillabaisse.
Facing page: Cheddar Cheese Soup (top) and Cream of Celery Soup (bottom).**

cook for 10 minutes on HIGH, stirring frequently, or until celery and shallot are soft. Stir in the flour and cook for 1 minute on HIGH. Add stock, milk, bay leaf, thyme and seasoning. Cover and cook for 18 minutes on HIGH, stirring frequently. Allow the soup to cool slightly. Remove bay leaf and thyme, and pour soup into a food processor. Purée until smooth, and return the soup to the bowl. Add celery seeds and re-heat for 2 minutes on HIGH. Just before serving, stir in the cream, and garnish with reserved celery leaves.

Cheddar Cheese Soup

PREPARATION TIME: 10 minutes

MICROWAVE COOKING TIME: 22 minutes

SERVES: 4 people

2 cups mature Cheddar cheese and Colby cheese, grated and mixed
1 carrot, peeled and diced
2 sticks celery, diced
3 tbsps butter
¼ cup flour
2 cups milk
1½ cups chicken or vegetable stock
1 bay leaf
¼ tsp thyme

GARNISH
Chopped parsley

Put butter, celery and carrot into a bowl. Cover with plastic wrap and pierce several times. Cook for 5 minutes on HIGH. Stir in the flour, and add the stock gradually, mixing well. Add thyme and bay leaf, and cook for 10 minutes on HIGH, uncovered. Add milk and cook for 5 minutes on HIGH. Put cheese into a bowl and stir in ½ cup of the liquid from the soup. Return cheese mixture to soup and cook, uncovered, for 2 minutes on HIGH. Serve with a garnish of chopped parsley.

Cream of Cucumber Soup

PREPARATION TIME: 10 minutes

MICROWAVE COOKING TIME: 22 minutes

SERVES: 4 people

1 large cucumber
1 shallot, finely chopped
2 tbsps butter
2 tbsps flour
1 cup chicken or vegetable stock
2 cups milk
½ cup light cream
1 tbsp chopped parsley
1 small clove garlic, crushed
1 bunch dill, finely chopped
Grated nutmeg
Salt
Pepper

Put butter, shallot and garlic into a large bowl. Cover with plastic wrap and pierce several times. Cook for 3 minutes on HIGH. Add flour and blend thoroughly. Wash cucumber, reserve 4 slices for garnish, and grate the rest. Add it to the bowl and cook for 5 minutes on HIGH, until cucumber is slightly softened. Stir in the stock, parsley, nutmeg, chopped dill and seasoning. Re-cover bowl and cook for 7 minutes on HIGH. Stir in the milk and cream and pour into a food processor. Purée until smooth and return to the bowl. Heat through for 3 minutes on HIGH and serve garnished with the cucumber slices. Serve hot or cold.

Clam Chowder

PREPARATION TIME: 15 minutes

MICROWAVE COOKING TIME: 16 minutes

SERVES: 4 people

1 quart clams
1 cup water, mixed with 1 tsp lemon juice
1 shallot, roughly chopped
4 strips green streaky bacon (rindless and boneless)
2 cups diced potatoes
1 onion, finely sliced
3¾ cups milk

2 tbsps butter
2 tbsps flour
Light cream as necessary
1 bay leaf
¼ tsp thyme
2 tbsps chopped parsley
Salt and pepper

GARNISH
Paprika

Scrub clams well and discard any that are open or broken. Put into a large bowl with the water, shallot and bay leaf. Cover with pierced plastic wrap and cook for 2 minutes on HIGH. Drain through a fine strainer and reserve. Remove clams from shells and set aside. Put butter, sliced onion and diced bacon into the rinsed-out bowl, cover, and cook on HIGH for 3 minutes. Stir in flour and cook a further 2 minutes on HIGH, stirring frequently. Add potatoes, milk, reserved clam liquid, thyme and seasoning. Cook for 10 minutes on HIGH, stirring occasionally. Add parsley and clams and, if soup is very thick, some cream to thin it down. Cook for 1 minute on HIGH. Serve sprinkled lightly with paprika.

Vichyssoise

PREPARATION TIME: 10-12 minutes

MICROWAVE COOKING TIME: 25 minutes

SERVES: 4 people

3 tbsps butter or margarine
3 leeks
2-3 medium potatoes, peeled and sliced
3 cups chicken or vegetable stock
⅓ cup sour cream
½ cup milk
Salt and pepper

Facing page: Clam Chowder (top) and Vichyssoise (bottom).

Trim the white part of the leeks, slice thinly and wash well. Shred the green part finely, wash well and set aside. Put butter into a large bowl and cook, uncovered, for about 1½ minutes on HIGH. Add potatoes and white part of leeks to the butter. Cover with plastic wrap and pierce several times. Cook for 5 minutes on HIGH, stirring frequently. Add half the stock, re-cover and cook on HIGH for about 14 minutes or until the vegetables are very soft. Cool slightly, pour into a food processor, and purée until smooth. Add remaining stock and milk, and adjust the seasoning. Put reserved green part of the leeks into a small bowl with 2-3 tbsps of water. Cover the bowl with plastic wrap and pierce several times. Cook for about 2 minutes on HIGH. Re-heat soup on HIGH for 3 minutes.

Add more milk if the soup is too thick. To serve, top with the soured cream and the thinly shredded green part of leeks. Serve hot or cold.

French Country Soup

PREPARATION TIME: 10 minutes

MICROWAVE COOKING TIME: 21 minutes

SERVES: 4 people

3 leeks, washed and sliced thinly
1 cup chopped carrots
2 cups diced potatoes
2 cups milk
2 cups chicken or vegetable stock
3 tbsps butter or margarine
1 bay leaf
1 sprig fresh rosemary

Salt
Pepper

GARNISH
Parsley leaves

Put leeks, potatoes, carrots and butter into a large bowl. Cover with plastic wrap, and pierce several times. Cook for 10 minutes on HIGH. Add milk, stock, bay leaf, sprig of rosemary and seasoning. Re-cover and cook for 7 minutes on HIGH. Leave standing, covered, for 1 minute. Put parsley leaves and 1 tbsp water into a small dish. Cover with plastic wrap and pierce several times. Cook on HIGH for 1 minute. Uncover the soup and allow it to cool slightly. Remove bay leaf and rosemary, pour soup into a food processor, and purée until smooth. Check seasoning and heat through for 3 minutes on HIGH. Serve with a garnish of parsley leaves.

Pumpkin Soup

PREPARATION TIME: 20 minutes

MICROWAVE COOKING TIME: 25 minutes

SERVES: 4-6 people

1 whole pumpkin, weighing about 2lbs
2 medium potatoes, peeled and sliced
2 small onions, finely chopped
2 tbsps butter
3 cups chicken stock
1 cup milk
½ cup heavy cream
½ tsp tarragon
½ tsp chopped parsley
Nutmeg
Salt
Pepper

GARNISH
1 small bunch chives

This page: Pumpkin Soup.
Facing page: French Country Soup.

Cut top off pumpkin and scoop out pulp and discard seeds. Push as much of the pulp as possible through a strainer. Using a small, sharp knife or tablespoon, remove pumpkin flesh from inside shell, leaving a ½″ lining of flesh. Put flesh, pulp, potatoes and onions into a large bowl with the butter. Cover with plastic wrap and pierce several times. Cook on HIGH for 10 minutes. Add stock, milk, thyme, parsley, nutmeg, and salt and pepper. Re-cover the bowl and cook on HIGH for 10 minutes. Pour the soup into a food processor and purée until smooth. Add heavy cream and mix in well. Wash pumpkin shell and top, and dry well. Return soup to the bowl and re-heat for 5 minutes on HIGH. Pour soup into cleaned pumpkin shell to serve, and garnish with chopped chives.

Watercress and Potato Soup

PREPARATION TIME: 10 minutes

MICROWAVE COOKING TIME: 22 minutes

SERVES: 4 people

1 bunch (about 2 cups) watercress
3 cups diced potatoes
1½ cups chicken or vegetable stock
1½ cups light cream, or milk
1 shallot, finely chopped
3 tbsps butter or margarine
Nutmeg
Lemon juice
Salt and pepper

Put the butter, shallot and potatoes into a large bowl. Cover with plastic wrap and pierce several times. Cook for about 2 minutes on HIGH. Add stock, salt and pepper, and pinch of nutmeg. Re-cover the bowl and cook on HIGH for about 10 minutes or until the vegetables are soft. Chop the watercress leaves, reserving 4 sprigs for garnish. Add the chopped leaves to the other ingredients in the bowl, re-cover and cook for another 2 minutes on HIGH. Put into a food processor and purée until smooth.

Return to the bowl. Stir in the cream and cook for 3-4 minutes on LOW until heated through. Do not allow the soup to boil. Stir in the lemon juice to taste, and adjust the seasoning. Serve the soup garnished with sprigs of watercress. Serve hot or cold.

Bean and Bacon Soup

PREPARATION TIME: 10 minutes

MICROWAVE COOKING TIME: 1 hour 35 minutes and 10 minutes standing time

SERVES: 4 people

½lb navy beans, picked over and washed
½lb smoked bacon
1 large onion, finely chopped
1 stalk celery, finely chopped
1 bay leaf
¼ tsp thyme
Pinch of sage
½ clove garlic, crushed
1 tbsp chopped parsley
Salt
Pepper

This page: Watercress and Potato Soup.
Facing page: Bean and Bacon Soup (top) and Cream of Onion Soup (bottom).

Put beans into a large casserole and add 4 cups water. Cover and cook for 10 minutes on HIGH, or until boiling. Allow to boil for 2 minutes, then set aside, covered, for 1 hour. Heat a browning dish for 5 minutes on HIGH and brown the bacon for 2 minutes. Crumble and set aside, reserving the fat. Put onion, celery, garlic and bacon fat into a large casserole and cook on HIGH for 2 minutes. Drain beans, and add to the casserole along with the thyme, sage and bay leaf. Pour on 4 cups of fresh water, cover, and cook for 45-55 minutes on HIGH. Then stir in the bacon, reserving 4 tbsps for garnish. Re-cover dish and cook a further 25-35 minutes on HIGH, or until beans are soft but not breaking apart. Add water as necessary during cooking. Allow to stand, covered, for 10 minutes. Remove the bay leaf and serve garnished with the reserved bacon.

Mulligatawny Soup

PREPARATION TIME: 12 minutes

MICROWAVE COOKING TIME:
36-38 minutes

SERVES: 4 people

1 cup onions, thinly sliced
2 apples, peeled and grated
4 tbsps butter
4 tbsps flour
1 tbsp tomato paste
2 tsps curry powder
1 tbsp mango chutney
⅓ cup quick-cooking rice
4 cups beef or chicken stock
1 small bunch fresh coriander leaves
1 bay leaf
1 clove garlic, crushed
Salt
Pepper

GARNISH
⅓ cup plain yogurt

Reserve 4 sprigs of coriander for garnish and chop 1 tbsp of the remainder. Put butter, onion and garlic into a large casserole. Cover and cook for 5 minutes on HIGH.

Blend in the flour and curry powder, then cover and cook for 2 minutes on HIGH. Add tomato paste, stock and 1 tbsp coriander, and cook for 5 minutes on HIGH until boiling. Add apple, chutney, rice and seasoning, and cook for 10 minutes on MEDIUM, or until rice is tender. Cook an additional 2 minutes on HIGH if necessary. Serve topped with yogurt and reserved coriander leaves.

Cream of Mushroom Soup

PREPARATION TIME: 10 minutes

MICROWAVE COOKING TIME:
17 minutes

SERVES: 4 people

¾lb mushrooms
1 shallot, finely chopped
2 cups chicken or vegetable stock
1½ cups milk
2 tbsps butter or margarine
3 tbsps flour
¼ tsp thyme
2 tbsps dry sherry
⅓ cup heavy cream
Salt
Pepper

Reserve 4 mushrooms to use as garnish, and chop the rest finely. Put them with the butter and shallot into a large glass bowl. Cover with plastic wrap and pierce several times. Cook for 4 minutes on HIGH or until mushrooms are soft. Stir occasionally. Add flour and stir well. Gradually add the stock, re-cover, and cook for 5 minutes on HIGH. Stir the mixture several times while cooking. Add milk, thyme and sherry, and cook on HIGH for 6 minutes, or until boiling. Stir several times during cooking. Allow the soup to stand for 1-2 minutes, covered. Slice remaining mushrooms thinly. Put them in a small bowl with 1 tbsp of water and a squeeze of lemon juice. Cover bowl with plastic wrap and pierce several times, and cook for 1 minute on HIGH. Add cream to the soup and cook for 2 minutes on HIGH. Serve

the soup garnished with the slices of mushroom.

Cream of Broccoli Soup

PREPARATION TIME: 10 minutes

MICROWAVE COOKING TIME:
20 minutes

SERVES: 4 people

1lb broccoli spears, fresh or frozen
2 tbsps butter
2 tbsps flour
1½ cups chicken or vegetable stock
2 cups milk
1 bay leaf
¼ tsp thyme
1 tbsp chopped parsley
½ cup heavy cream
Salt
Pepper

Chop broccoli roughly, reserving 4-8 small flowerets for garnish. Put chopped broccoli into a loosely tied roasting bag with 2 tbsps water. Cook on HIGH for 5 minutes. (The broccoli may also be cooked in a bowl covered with pierced plastic wrap.) Put butter into a large bowl and cook for 1 minute on HIGH. Stir in the flour, and add the milk, stock, thyme, parsley, bay leaf and seasoning. Cook for 7 minutes on HIGH, stirring several times. Add broccoli and cook a further 3 minutes on HIGH. Pour the soup into a food processor and purée until smooth. Put reserved flowerets of broccoli into a small bowl with 1 tbsp of water. Cover with pierced plastic wrap and cook for 2 minutes on HIGH. Set aside. Add cream and re-heat the soup for 2 minutes on HIGH. Serve with a garnish of broccoli flowerets.

Facing page: Cream of Mushroom Soup (top) and Mulligatawny Soup (bottom).

Cream of Onion Soup

PREPARATION TIME: 10 minutes

MICROWAVE COOKING TIME:
18 minutes

SERVES: 4 people

1½lbs onions, finely chopped
2 tbsps butter
2 tbsps flour
2 cups beef or chicken stock
1½ cups milk
1 tbsp Madeira
½ cup cream

GARNISH
4 green onions, sliced

Put the butter into a large bowl and cook for 1 minute on HIGH. Add onions, and cook for 5 minutes on HIGH, stirring occasionally until light brown. Stir in the flour, stock, bay leaf, and salt and pepper. Cook for 10 minutes on HIGH. Pour the soup into a food processor and purée until smooth. Pour milk into a small bowl and heat for 2 minutes on HIGH. Pour the soup back into a bowl, add the milk, and stir well. Re-heat on HIGH for 2 minutes and add the Madeira. Stir in the cream before serving and garnish with the sliced green onions.

Creamy Borscht

PREPARATION TIME: 15 minutes

MICROWAVE COOKING TIME:
27 minutes

SERVES: 4 people

3 beets, grated
1½ cups cabbage, shredded
1 medium carrot, thinly sliced
2 medium potatoes, peeled and thinly sliced
1 medium onion, finely chopped
1 small clove garlic, crushed
1 teaspoon tomato paste
½ cup cream

3 cups beef stock
¼ cup white wine
1 bunch dill
1 bay leaf
Salt
Pepper

GARNISH
½ cup sour cream

Reserve 4 sprigs of dill for garnish and chop the rest. Put the dill, carrot, onion, potatoes, cabbage, garlic, bay leaf, seasoning, and half the stock into a large casserole. Cover and cook on HIGH for 15 minutes or until vegetables soften. Add the remaining stock, beets, wine and tomato paste, and cover and cook on HIGH for 10 minutes. Stir occasionally. Remove bay leaf. Pour soup into a food processor and purée until smooth. Add cream and blend thoroughly. Return soup to bowl and re-heat for 2 minutes on HIGH. Serve topped with sour cream and sprigs of dill.

Stilton Cheese and Walnut Soup

PREPARATION TIME: 10 minutes

MICROWAVE COOKING TIME:
18 minutes

SERVES: 4 people

2 cups Stilton cheese, crumbled (half Cheddar and half blue cheese may be substituted)
1 large onion, finely chopped
3 tbsps butter
2 tbsps flour
1½ cups chicken stock
1½ cups milk
¼ cup cream
½ cup walnuts, finely chopped
1 bay leaf
1 sprig thyme
Salt and pepper

**This page: Creamy Borscht.
Facing page: Cream of Broccoli Soup (top) and Stilton Cheese and Walnut Soup (bottom).**

Jerusalem Artichoke and Almond Soup

PREPARATION TIME: 15 minutes

MICROWAVE COOKING TIME:
33-38 minutes

**CONVENTIONAL
OVEN TEMPERATURE:**
350°F, 180°C

SERVES: 4 people

2½ lbs Jerusalem artichoke
2 shallots, finely chopped
¼ cup blanched almonds
2 tbsps butter or margarine
1 cup chicken stock
1½ cups milk
½ cup heavy cream
¼ cup white wine
1 bay leaf
Grated nutmeg
Lemon juice
Salt
Pepper

GARNISH
¼ cup sliced almonds, browned

Peel artichokes and keep in a bowl of cold water and lemon juice. Thinly slice them and put them into a bowl with shallots, butter and almonds. Cover with plastic wrap and pierce several times, and cook for 4 minutes on HIGH. Pour in the stock and wine, add the bay leaf, grated nutmeg and seasoning, and cook, uncovered, for 10 minutes on HIGH. Remove bay leaf, add cream and milk, and pour into a food processor. Purée until smooth and adjust seasoning. Meanwhile, brown almonds for garnish in a conventional oven for 15 minutes or in a microwave-convection oven on Combination for 7 minutes, stirring often. Re-heat soup for 2 minutes on HIGH, and serve garnished with the browned almonds and more grated nutmeg.

Put onion and butter into a large bowl. Cover with plastic wrap and pierce several times. Cook for 6 minutes on HIGH. Stir in flour, add the stock gradually and mix well. Add bay leaf, thyme, salt and pepper, and cook, uncovered, for 10 minutes on HIGH. Remove the herbs. Crumble the cheese into a bowl and add ½ cup of the soup to the cheese. Stir in well. Return cheese mixture to the rest of the soup and add cream. Cook 1 minute, uncovered, on HIGH. Add the walnuts to the bowl, reserving about 2 tbsps for garnish. Cook on HIGH for 1 minute. Serve garnished with the reserved walnuts.

This page: Jerusalem Artichoke and Almond Soup (top) and Cream of Carrot and Orange Soup (bottom). Facing page: Spiced Tomato Soup (top) and Green Pea Soup (bottom).

Green Pea Soup

PREPARATION TIME: 10 minutes

MICROWAVE COOKING TIME:
12 minutes

SERVES: 4 people

1lb frozen peas
2 tbsps butter
2 tbsps flour
1 cup chicken or vegetable stock
1½ cups milk
½ cup light cream
1 shallot, finely chopped
1 small bunch fresh mint
¼ tsp marjoram
1 tbsp chopped parsley
Salt
Pepper

Put butter and shallot into a large bowl and cover with pierced plastic wrap. Cook for 5 minutes on HIGH, then add the peas to the bowl, reserving ½ cup. Add the stock, milk, marjoram, parsley and seasoning. Cook for 5 minutes on HIGH. Pour into a food processor and purée until smooth. Chop the mint, reserving 4-8 leaves for garnish, if desired. Return soup to the bowl, and add chopped mint, cream and reserved peas. Re-heat soup for 2 minutes on HIGH. Garnish with the mint leaves.

Cream of Lettuce Soup

PREPARATION TIME: 10 minutes

MICROWAVE COOKING TIME:
18 minutes

SERVES: 4 people

2-3 potatoes, peeled and diced
1 onion, finely chopped
1 head romaine lettuce
1 cup chicken stock
2 cups milk
2 tbsps butter or margarine
½ cup cream
Ground nutmeg
¼ tsp thyme
1 tsp chopped parsley
Salt
Pepper

Put potatoes and onion into a large bowl with the butter and stock. Cover with plastic wrap and pierce several times. Cook on HIGH for 10 minutes. Wash lettuce well and shred leaves finely, reserving a small amount for garnish. Add to the bowl with the seasoning, thyme and ground nutmeg, and cook for 1 minute on HIGH. Add the milk and pour the soup into a food processor, and purée until smooth. Add the cream. Return to the bowl and re-heat for 7 minutes on HIGH. Serve soup garnished with reserved shredded lettuce. Serve hot or cold.

Spiced Tomato Soup

PREPARATION TIME: 10 minutes

MICROWAVE COOKING TIME:
22 minutes

SERVES: 4 people

28oz can tomatoes
2 onions, finely chopped
2 cups beef stock
1 tbsp cornstarch
1 tbsp tomato paste
¼ cup port or brandy
1 tsp thyme
½ stick cinnamon
2 whole cloves
3 black peppercorns
3 allspice berries
1 bay leaf
Salt
Sugar

GARNISH
2 tomatoes
4 tbsps heavy cream

Put tomatoes and their juice, stock, onion, herbs, spices and salt into a large bowl. Cook, uncovered, for 20 minutes on HIGH. Add a pinch of sugar if necessary, to bring out the tomato flavor. Sieve tomatoes, extracting as much pulp as possible. Blend cornstarch and port and stir into the soup. Put tomatoes for garnish into a bowl of water and cook on HIGH for 1 minute. Drain and put into cold water. Peel, remove seeds, cut into thin shreds and set aside. Return soup to oven and cook, uncovered, for 2 minutes on HIGH, stirring often. Adjust seasoning, and serve soup garnished with a swirl of heavy cream and the shreds of tomato.

Cream of Carrot and Orange Soup

PREPARATION TIME: 10 minutes

MICROWAVE COOKING TIME:
18 minutes

SERVES: 4 people

3 cups grated carrots
1 shallot, finely chopped
2 tbsps butter or margarine
1 cup chicken or vegetable stock
2 cups milk
⅓ cup heavy cream
Juice and rind of 1 orange
1 bay leaf
1 sprig of thyme
1 small bunch chives, chopped
Salt
Pepper

Pare the rind from the orange and squeeze the juice. Put butter into a large bowl and heat for 1 minute on HIGH. Add onion and cook for 5 minutes on HIGH. Add carrots, stock, bay leaf, thyme, and salt and pepper. Cover with pierced plastic wrap and cook for 10 minutes on HIGH. Add milk, orange juice and orange rind and cook for 1 minute on HIGH. Remove bay leaf, thyme, and orange rind, and pour into a food processor. Purée until smooth. Return soup to bowl, and heat through for 2 minutes on HIGH. Stir in the chives and the cream before serving. Serve hot or cold.

Facing page: Cream of Lettuce Soup.

VEGETABLE AND PASTA SOUPS

Chicken Vegetable Soup

PREPARATION TIME: 15 minutes

MICROWAVE COOKING TIME:
23 minutes

SERVES: 4 people

1lb chicken parts
4 cups water
1 chicken bouillon cube
1 small turnip, diced
1 onion, finely chopped
3 sticks celery, sliced
2 medium carrots, diced
¼ cup frozen peas
¼ cup fresh or frozen sliced green beans
½ cup mushrooms, quartered
¼ tsp thyme
1 bay leaf
1 tbsp chopped parsley

Put the chicken parts and the water into a large casserole with the thyme, bay leaf and seasoning. Cover and cook on HIGH for 15 minutes. Remove chicken and leave to cool. Remove the skin and bones and cut the chicken into small pieces. Set aside. Strain stock. Return stock to casserole and skim any fat from the surface. Taste and, if necessary, add the bouillon cube. Add the carrot, onion, celery and turnip; cover and cook for 10 minutes on HIGH. At this stage, if using fresh beans, cut into even sized lengths and add to the stock with the mushrooms. Cover and cook for 4 minutes on HIGH. Add frozen peas and parsley and cook a further 1 minute on HIGH. (If using frozen beans, add with the peas.) Add chicken. Adjust seasoning, and heat through for 3 minutes on HIGH. Serve.

Greek Lemon Soup

PREPARATION TIME: 8 minutes

MICROWAVE COOKING TIME:
17 minutes

SERVES: 4 people

3 lemons
1 onion, finely chopped
3 tbsps butter or margarine
2 tbsps flour
1 cup quick-cooking rice
4 cups chicken stock
¼ tsp powdered oregano
Nutmeg
Salt
Pepper

Put butter and onion into a bowl. Cover with plastic wrap and pierce several times. Cook on HIGH for about 3 minutes. Add flour to bowl and cook on HIGH for an additional 1½-2 minutes. Gradually stir in the stock. Grate rind and squeeze juice from 2 lemons, and add to the bowl with the bay leaf, pinch of nutmeg, oregano, salt and pepper. Cook on HIGH for 5 minutes. Add rice, re-cover the bowl, and cook for 5 minutes on HIGH, stirring frequently. Additional cooking time may be needed if the rice is not tender. Leave to stand, covered, about 2 minutes. Slice remaining lemon thinly and garnish each serving of soup with a slice of lemon.

Minestrone

PREPARATION TIME: 15 minutes

MICROWAVE COOKING TIME:
26 minutes

SERVES: 4 people

2 small leeks, washed and cut into thin strips
2 tbsps oil
1½ cups canned tomatoes
1 green pepper, sliced
7oz can canellini, or haricot, beans
1 carrot, cut into 1" strips
2 sticks celery, cut into 1" strips
1 zucchini, cut into 1" strips
1 clove garlic, crushed
¼ lb ham, cut into thin strips
4 cups stock (preferably ham)
⅓ cup macaroni
1 bay leaf
½ tsp basil
½ tsp oregano
½ tsp fennel seed
Salt and pepper
Sugar

GARNISH
½ cup Parmesan cheese, grated

Put oil, leeks, carrot, celery, garlic and herbs in a large casserole. Cover and cook 6 minutes on HIGH. Add macaroni, tomatoes and their juice, stock, ham, drained beans, salt, pepper and a pinch of sugar, and cook, covered, on HIGH for 6 minutes. Add zucchini, green pepper and parsley, and cook 5 minutes on HIGH, or until pasta is tender. Serve with grated Parmesan cheese.

Facing page: Minestrone.

Cream of Asparagus Soup

PREPARATION TIME: 10 minutes

MICROWAVE COOKING TIME:
32 minutes

SERVES: 4 people

1lb asparagus, fresh or frozen
3 tbsps butter or margarine
3 tbsps flour
1 shallot, finely chopped
3 cups chicken stock
½ cup cream
1 bay leaf
¼ tsp thyme
Salt
Pepper
Nutmeg

Place butter and shallot into a large casserole. Cover and cook on HIGH for 6 minutes. Stir in the flour and cook a further 1 minute on HIGH. Stir in the stock and cook for 15 minutes on HIGH, until boiling. Chop asparagus roughly and, if using fresh, reserve 4 tips for garnish. Add asparagus, bay leaf, seasoning, and a pinch of grated nutmeg, and cook for 10 minutes on MEDIUM. Remove the bay leaf, and pour the soup into a food processor and purée until smooth. Put reserved asparagus tips into a small bowl with 1 tbsp of water. Cover with plastic wrap and pierce several times. Cook for 1 minute on HIGH and set aside. Add the cream to the soup, cover, and re-heat for 2-3 minutes. Serve garnished with the reserved asparagus tips and more grated nutmeg.

French Onion Soup

PREPARATION TIME: 10 minutes

MICROWAVE COOKING TIME:
27 minutes

SERVES: 4 people

1½ lbs onions, thinly sliced
4 tbsps butter or margarine
2 tbsps flour
½ cup dry cider or white wine
2 tbsps Calvados or brandy

4 cups beef stock
¼ tbsp thyme
1 bay leaf
4 slices French bread, toasted and
  buttered
½ cup Gruyère or Swiss cheese
Salt
Pepper

Place onions, butter, salt and pepper into a large bowl and cook on HIGH for 8 minutes. Stir occasionally. Stir in the flour, add the stock, cider, Calvados, thyme and bay leaf. Cover bowl with plastic wrap and pierce several times. Cook on HIGH for 10 minutes. Uncover and stir occasionally. Reduce the setting to LOW and cook a further 8 minutes.

Leave the bowl to stand covered for 1-2 minutes. Put slices of toast on a plate, and sprinkle over the grated cheese thickly. Cook on LOW until cheese starts to melt, and then broil conventionally until lightly browned. Spoon the soup into individual micro-proof bowls. Top each with the cheese toast and heat through for 1 minute on HIGH. Serve immediately.

This page: Chicken Vegetable Soup. Facing page: Cream of Asparagus Soup (top) and French Onion Soup (bottom).

and add them to the bowl with the sesame seed oil. Heat soup through for 2 minutes on HIGH. Serve garnished with more chopped green onion if desired.

Potato Soup

PREPARATION TIME: 10 minutes

MICROWAVE COOKING TIME: 21 minutes

SERVES: 4 people

4 cups diced potatoes
3 tbsps butter or margarine
1 onion, thinly sliced
1 cup water
3 cups milk
1 bay leaf
1 sprig of thyme
Salt
Pepper
Nutmeg

GARNISH
½ cup Colby cheese, grated

Put potatoes, onions and butter into a large bowl. Cover with plastic wrap and pierce several times. Cook for 10 minutes on HIGH. Add milk, water, thyme, bay leaf, seasoning and grated nutmeg, and cook for 7 minutes on HIGH. Leave standing, covered, for 1 minute. Uncover and allow to cool slightly. Remove bay leaf and thyme, pour soup into a food processor, and purée until smooth. Check seasoning and consistency. If too thick, add more milk. Cover and heat through for 3 minutes on HIGH. Serve garnished with the grated cheese.

Chinese Chicken and Mushroom Soup

PREPARATION TIME: 8 minutes

MICROWAVE COOKING TIME: 36 minutes

SERVES: 4 people

6 dried Chinese mushrooms
2 chicken breasts
1 cup water
1 small can water chestnuts, sliced
1 small can bamboo shoots, sliced
1 bunch green onions, sliced diagonally
¼lb fine Chinese egg noodles
¼lb pea pods
1 tbsp light soy sauce
2 tbsps dry sherry
1 tsp sesame seed oil
1 tbsp cornstarch
3 cups chicken stock
Salt and pepper

Put mushrooms into a small bowl and cover with cold water. Cover bowl with plastic wrap and pierce several times. Heat on HIGH for 2 minutes and leave to stand. Put chicken breasts into a bowl with 1 cup water. Cover with pierced plastic wrap and cook for 15 minutes on HIGH. Put noodles into a bowl with 2 pints water. Cover with pierced plastic wrap and cook for 3 minutes on HIGH. Leave standing, covered, for 5 minutes. Drain and slice mushrooms, and put into a large bowl with the stock. Cover with pierced plastic wrap and cook for 1 minute on HIGH. Skin, bone and shred chicken and add to bowl with green onions, pea pods, water chestnuts and bamboo shoots and cook for 1 minute on HIGH. Mix cornstarch, soy sauce and sherry with a tbsp of the hot liquid. Pour into the bowl with the rest of the soup and cook, stirring several times, for 5 minutes on HIGH. Drain noodles

This page: Potato Soup (top) and Greek Lemon Soup (bottom). Facing page: Chinese Chicken and Mushroom Soup.

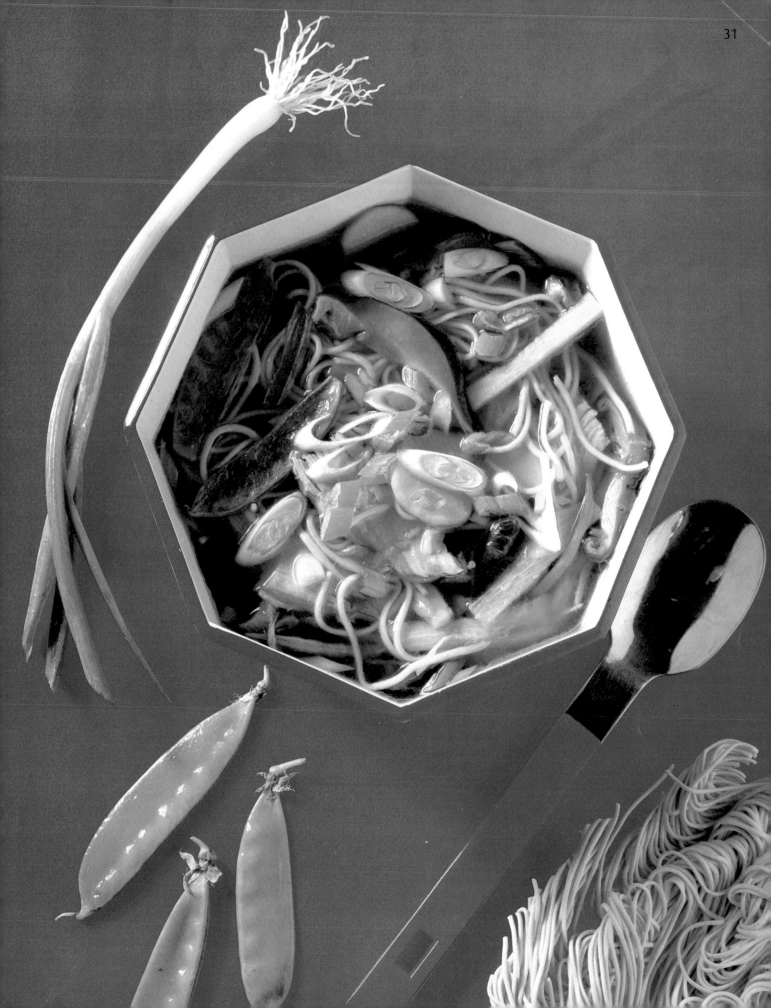

Chili Corn Chowder

PREPARATION TIME: 15 minutes

MICROWAVE COOKING TIME:
24 minutes

SERVES: 4 people

3 tbsps butter or margarine
1 shallot, finely chopped
4 strips smoked bacon (rindless and
*   boneless)*
3 tbsps flour
2 cups chicken stock
1½ cups milk
2 medium potatoes, peeled and cut into
*   ½" dice*
1 red pepper, diced
1 green chili pepper, finely chopped
1½ cups corn, frozen
½ cup light cream
1 tbsp chopped parsley
¼ tsp ground cumin
1 bay leaf

GARNISH
4 green onions

Put butter into a bowl and cook for 1 minute on HIGH. Dice bacon and add it with the shallot to the butter. Cover with pierced plastic wrap and cook for 5 minutes on HIGH until onions are softened. Stir in the flour and cumin, and cook for 1 minute on HIGH. Gradually stir in the stock and milk, and add potatoes and bay leaf. Cook for 6 minutes on HIGH or until boiling. Add red pepper and as much of the chili pepper as desired. Cook for 10 minutes or until potatoes soften. Remove bay leaf, add corn, cream, parsley and seasoning, and cook for 3 minutes on HIGH. Serve garnished with chopped green onion.

Italian Onion Soup

PREPARATION TIME: 10 minutes

MICROWAVE COOKING TIME:
16-23 minutes and 1-2 minutes
standing time

SERVES: 4 people

1½lbs onions, thinly sliced
16oz can plum tomatoes

3 tbsps butter or margarine
2 tbsps flour
½ cup red wine
1½ cups beef stock
¼ tsp basil
¼ tsp oregano
1 bay leaf
Salt
Pepper
Tomato paste
4 slices French bread, toasted and
*   buttered*
2 tbsps Parmesan cheese, grated
2 tbsps Cheddar cheese, grated

Place onions, butter, salt and pepper into a large bowl and cook on HIGH for 6 minutes. Stir occasionally. Stir in flour, add the stock, tomatoes, red wine, basil, oregano and bay leaf. Cover the bowl with plastic wrap and pierce several times. Cook on HIGH for 8 minutes. Uncover and stir occasionally. Reduce setting to LOW and cook for a further 4

minutes. Leave the bowl to stand covered for 1-2 minutes. Adjust seasoning and add tomato paste, if necessary, for color and flavor. Mix the cheeses together, put the slices of toast on a plate, and sprinkle over the grated cheese. Cook on LOW until cheese starts to melt, and then broil conventionally until lightly browned. Use the Combination setting on convection microwave oven for 7 minutes. Spoon the soup into individual micro-proof bowls. Top each with the cheese toast and heat through for 1 minute on HIGH.

This page: Chili Corn Chowder. Facing page: Curried Cauliflower Soup (top) and Italian Onion Soup (bottom).

Curried Cauliflower Soup

PREPARATION TIME: 10 minutes

MICROWAVE COOKING TIME:
15 minutes

SERVES: 4 people

*4 cups cauliflowerets, or 1 small
    cauliflower cut into flowerets*
2 shallots finely chopped
2 tbsps butter or margarine
2 tbsps flour
2 tsps curry powder
1½ cups chicken or vegetable stock
2 cups milk
Salt
Pepper

GARNISH
⅓ cup sliced almonds, browned

Put cauliflowerets into a roasting bag
with the shallot and bay leaf. Tie bag
loosely and cook for 8 minutes on
HIGH. (Cauliflower may also be
cooked in a bowl covered with
pierced plastic wrap.) Put butter into
a large bowl and cook for 1 minute
on HIGH until melted. Stir in the
curry powder and flour, and cook for
1 minute on HIGH. Add milk and
cook for 3 minutes on HIGH, stirring
occasionally. Pour the soup into a
food processor, add the cauliflower,
and purée until smooth. Return the
soup to the oven to heat through for
2 minutes on HIGH. Serve garnished
with the browned sliced almonds.

Vegetable Soup

PREPARATION TIME: 10 minutes

MICROWAVE COOKING TIME:
21 minutes

SERVES: 4 people

1 large carrot, peeled and diced
1 large turnip, peeled and diced
2 leeks, washed and sliced thinly
2 potatoes, peeled and diced
¼ cup frozen peas
¼ cup frozen corn
½ cup fresh or frozen sliced green beans
¼lb okra (optional)
16oz can plum tomatoes

2 cups chicken or vegetable stock
⅓ cup soup pasta
1 bay leaf
¼ tsp marjoram or savory
1 tbsp chopped parsley
Pepper

Put butter into a large bowl and cook
for 45 seconds on HIGH until it
melts. Add carrots, turnips, leeks and
potatoes and mix together. Cover
with plastic wrap and pierce several
times. Cook on HIGH for 10 minutes
or until vegetables begin to soften.
Stir occasionally. Add stock,
tomatoes, bay leaf, marjoram, pasta,
salt and pepper. Cover and cook for
7 minutes on HIGH. Slice beans (if

fresh), trim okra, and slice into
rounds, and add to bowl. Re-cover
bowl and cook for 2 minutes on
HIGH. Add corn, peas and parsley.
Cook for 1 minute on HIGH or until
pasta is tender. Sprinkle with more
chopped parsley, if desired, before
serving.

**This page: Vegetable Soup.
Facing page: Jellied Vegetable
Terrine with Tomato Dressing.**

SOUPS AND APPETIZERS

TARTS, TERRINES AND PÂTÉS

Jellied Vegetable Terrine with Tomato Dressing

PREPARATION TIME: 15 minutes

MICROWAVE COOKING TIME: 11 minutes

SERVES: 4 people

TERRINE
1 tbsp gelatine
1 chicken bouillon cube
2 cups boiling water (less 2 tbsps)
2 tbsps dry sherry
8oz green beans, ends trimmed
1 large carrot, peeled
1-2 Jerusalem artichokes, peeled
4oz mushrooms, cleaned
½ cup frozen peas

DRESSING
14oz can tomato sauce
1 tsp tomato paste
Juice and grate rind of half a lemon
¼ tsp chives, snipped
¼ tsp parsley, chopped
¼ tsp thyme, chopped
¼ tsp basil, chopped
3-4 tbsps olive oil
2 tbsps red wine vinegar
¼ tsp Dijon mustard
1 bay leaf
Sugar
Salt
Pepper

GARNISH
1 bunch watercress

Heat water in a glass measuring cup for 3-4 minutes on HIGH until boiling. Add sherry and stir in the gelatine and bouillon cube. Leave to cool at room temperature, then put into a bowl of cold water. The aspic must be cold but liquid. If it sets too quickly in the cup, melt again for 1-2 minutes on HIGH. Then chill again in the cold water, and repeat the process again when necessary. Leave green beans whole and cook for 8 minutes on HIGH with 2 tbsps water in a small, shallow dish covered with pierced plastic wrap. Cut carrots lengthwise into ¼" sticks and cook for 10 minutes in the same way as the beans. Cut artichokes into thin rounds and cook for 8 minutes.

Chicken and Asparagus Terrine with Lemon Mousseline Sauce

PREPARATION TIME: 15 minutes

MICROWAVE COOKING TIME: 33 minutes

SERVES: 4-6 people

TERRINE
1lb chicken breasts
1½ cups cream
12oz low-fat cheese
2 tbsps white wine
½ cup water
3 eggs
1lb asparagus spears, fresh or frozen
Salt
Pepper
Nutmeg
1 bay leaf

SAUCE
½ cup butter
3 egg yolks
Rind and juice of 1 lemon
¼ cup whipping cream
1 bay leaf
1 blade mace
Salt
Pepper

Cut tips off asparagus spears, trim stalk ends, and cook on HIGH for 6 minutes with 2 tbsps water in a shallow dish covered with pierced plastic wrap. Leave to cool. Put chicken breasts into a bowl with the white wine, water and bay leaf. Cover with pierced plastic wrap and cook for 15 minutes on HIGH. Cool and remove skin and bones. Put chicken, cheese, seasoning, nutmeg and 2 eggs into a food processor, and purée until smooth. In a clean bowl, purée the asparagus spears with 1 egg, salt and pepper. Put half the chicken mixture into a loaf pan and smooth evenly. Cover with half the asparagus mixture and layer on the reserved asparagus tips. Cover with remaining

This page: Chicken and Asparagus Terrine with Lemon Mousseline Sauce.
Facing page: Tomato Tarts Niçoise (top) and Cheese and Mushroom Tarts (bottom).

Remove stalks from mushrooms and slice caps thinly. Cook them for 3 minutes on HIGH, then the frozen peas for 1 minute on HIGH. Dampen a 1lb loaf pan with water and pour in a ¼" layer of cool aspic. Chill until set. Arrange a layer of peas on top and pour over a thin layer of aspic to set the peas in place. Chill until set, then add more aspic to just cover the peas. Chill again until set. Repeat the process with a layer of artichokes, green beans, carrots and mushrooms. Fill the pan to the top with aspic and chill for 1-2 hours until firm. Meanwhile, put tomato sauce, paste,

garlic, bay leaf, seasoning and sugar into a bowl. Cover with pierced plastic wrap and cook for 10 minutes on HIGH, stirring frequently. Allow sauce to cool completely. Whisk oil, vinegar and mustard together until thick. Whisk in the tomato sauce, add chopped herbs, and adjust seasoning. Unmold the terrine and cut into ½" slices. Serve with tomato dressing and small bouquets of watercress or parsley.

asparagus mixture, then the remaining chicken mixture. Cover the dish with plastic wrap and cook for 10 minutes on HIGH. Cover and weight down the top, leaving to stand for 5 minutes. Serve hot with the lemon mousseline sauce.

To make sauce: Put the butter into a glass measuring cup or a small, deep bowl and cook for 1 minute on HIGH to melt. Put lemon juice, bay leaf and mace into another bowl and heat for 1 minute on HIGH. Beat egg yolks, lemon rind and seasoning, and strain on the juice. Pour egg yolk mixture into the butter and stir well. Have a bowl of ice water ready. Put the sauce mixture into the oven and cook for 15 seconds on HIGH. Remove and stir, repeating the process until sauce has thickened – approximately 2 minutes. Put the jug immediately into the ice water to stop the cooking. Whip cream, fold into the sauce and serve at once with the terrine.

Country Pâté

PREPARATION TIME: 10 minutes

MICROWAVE COOKING TIME:
15 minutes

SERVES: 6-8 people

½ lb ground pork
½ lb ground veal
¼ lb ham, ground
¼ lb pork liver
3oz ground pork fat
1 clove garlic, crushed
4 tbsps brandy
Ground allspice
Thyme
1 bay leaf
2 tsps green peppercorns in brine, rinsed
8 slices bacon, bones and rind removed
Salt
Pepper

Line a 1lb glass loaf dish with the bacon. Remove skin and ducts from liver, grind in a food processor, and mix with the ground meats, garlic, herbs, spices, brandy, peppercorns and seasoning. Press meat mixture into the dish on top of bacon. Place

bay leaf on top. Fold edges of bacon over the top and cover with plastic wrap. Put a custard cup of water into the oven with the pâté, and cook on MEDIUM for 6 minutes. Leave to stand for 5 minutes and cook for a further 10 minutes on MEDIUM. Cover with foil, press down and weight. Leave to chill 2-4 hours. Remove the bay leaf, and cut mixture into thin slices (about 18) to serve.

Asparagus with Orange Hollandaise

PREPARATION TIME: 10 minutes

MICROWAVE COOKING TIME:
11 minutes

SERVES: 4 people

2lbs asparagus spears
½ cup butter
3 egg yolks
Juice of half a lemon
Grated rind and juice of ½ an orange
1 small bay leaf
1 blade mace
Salt
Pepper

Trim any thick ends from the asparagus spears and rinse them well. Put into a shallow casserole with 3-4 tbsps water. Cover and cook for 7 minutes until just tender. Leave covered while preparing sauce. Put the butter in a glass measuring cup or jug, or small, deep bowl and cook for 1 minute on HIGH to melt. Put orange juice, lemon juice, bay leaf and mace into another bowl and heat for 1 minute on HIGH. Beat egg yolks, orange rind and seasoning together, and strain on the juice. Pour egg yolk mixture into the butter and stir well to mix. Have a bowl of ice water on hand. Put the sauce mixture into the oven and cook for 15 seconds on HIGH. Remove and stir well, and repeat the process until sauce is thickened. It should take about 2 minutes. Put the jug immediately into the ice water to prevent sauce from cooking further. Serve at once with the asparagus.

Cheese and Mushroom Tarts

PREPARATION TIME: 10 minutes

MICROWAVE COOKING TIME:
11 minutes

SERVES: 4 people

1½ cups wholewheat crackers
½ cup butter or margarine
½ cup Cheddar cheese, grated
½ lb mushrooms, roughly chopped
4 tbsps chopped chives
1 tbsp flour
1 tbsp butter
⅓ cup chicken or vegetable stock
1 egg, beaten
2 tbsps light cream
½ cup Colby cheese, grated
Cayenne pepper
Salt
Pepper

Crush the crackers into a food processor and grate in the cheese. Melt ⅓ cup of the butter on HIGH for 1 minute and pour into the crumbs and cheese. Process to mix. Press the mixture firmly into 8 individual tart pans or a muffin pan. Cook for 2 minutes on HIGH, and cool. Melt the remaining butter on HIGH. Mix in flour, chives, seasoning and stock, and cook for 2 minutes on HIGH, or until sauce has thickened. Fill the tart shells with the mushrooms. Beat egg, cream, Cayenne pepper and seasonings together until frothy. Fold in the Colby cheese. Pour on top of the mushroom filling and cook for 2 minutes on HIGH until the cheese sets. Tops may be browned under a broiler if desired, or cooked for 5 minutes on the Combination setting in a microwave-convection oven. Serve immediately.

Facing page: Country Pâté (top) and Asparagus with Orange Hollandaise (bottom).

Press mixture firmly onto the ham. Cover with plastic wrap and cook for 6 minutes on MEDIUM. Leave to stand for 5 minutes, then cook for a further 7 minutes on MEDIUM. Cover with foil and weight down the top. Leave to chill for 4-5 hours, and serve with tarragon sauce.

To make sauce: Have ready a bowl of ice water. Beat egg and sugar in a small glass bowl until creamy. Add vinegar and cook on HIGH for 30 seconds. Remove and stir. Repeat the process until sauce thickens (approximately 2 minutes). Put immediately into ice water to stop the cooking, and leave to go cold, stirring occasionally. Whip the cream and fold into the sauce with the chopped tarragon.

Tomato Tarts Niçoise

PREPARATION TIME: 20 minutes

MICROWAVE COOKING TIME: 10 minutes

SERVES: 4 people

PASTRY
1 cup flour
1½ tbsps butter or margarine
1½ tbsps baking powder
⅓ cup milk
Pinch salt
1 tbsp chopped parsley, basil and thyme, mixed

FILLING
1 onion, finely slicd
½ lb tomatoes, skinned and thickly sliced
1 tbsp olive oil
16 black olives, stoned
1 tbsp capers
8 anchovies
¼ tsp oregano or basil
½ cup Gruyère cheese, grated

To make pastry: Sift flour with salt and cut in the butter until mixture resembles fine breadcrumbs. Add herbs and milk, and mix to a soft dough. It may not be necessary to add all the milk. Turn out and knead lightly. Divide dough into 4 pieces and roll each out to line a muffin pan or 8 tart pans.

Terrine of Duck and Cherries with Tarragon Sauce

PREPARATION TIME: 15 minutes

MICROWAVE COOKING TIME: 15 minutes

SERVES: 6-8 people

TERRINE
1 5lb duck, skinned and boned
6 slices boiled ham
⅓ cup ground pork
⅓ cup ground veal
½ clove garlic, crushed
8oz can cherries, drained and pitted
4 tbsps white wine
Allspice
2 tsps tarragon, chopped
1 tbsp kirsch
Salt
Pepper

SAUCE
1 egg
3 tbsps tarragon vinegar
¼ tsp chopped fresh tarragon
2 tbsps sugar
½ cup whipping cream

To prepare terrine: Grind duck meat in a food processor and mix with pork and veal. Add garlic, kirsch, wine, tarragon, allspice and seasoning. Fold in the cherries. Line a 1lb glass loaf dish with the ham slices.

Facing page: Terrine of Duck and Cherries with Tarragon Sauce. This page: Ham and Mushroom Pâté (left) and Stuffed Tomatoes Provençal (right).

To make filling and assemble tarts: Bring 2 cups water to the boil for 3 minutes on HIGH. Put in the tomatoes for 5 seconds, remove and plunge them into cold water. Peel, drain and slice them. Put olive oil in a bowl, add onion, and cook for 3 minutes on HIGH or until softened. Season, mix with half the cheese. Put into the bottom of each pastry shell. Layer tomatoes, seasoning and sprinkling the herbs between each layer. Decorate with anchovies,

capers and olives, and sprinkle with remaining cheese. Bake for 4 minutes on HIGH, turning pans once. Brown under a broiler if desired. Do not overbake or pastry will become hard.

Ham and Mushroom Pâté

PREPARATION TIME: 10 minutes

MICROWAVE COOKING TIME: 20 minutes

SERVES: 6-8 people

1lb cooked ham, minced
1 cup fresh white breadcrumbs
3 eggs
3 tbsps butter
4oz mushrooms, finely chopped

1 shallot, finely chopped
1 clove garlic, crushed
2 tbsps dry sherry
¼ tsp thyme
¼ tsp parsley
Nutmeg
Salt and pepper

Melt the butter in a small bowl and add the shallot. Cover with pierced plastic wrap and cook for 2 minutes on HIGH. Add the thyme, parsley and mushrooms, and cook for a further 4 minutes, uncovered, on HIGH. Add the seasoning and ¼ cup of the breadcrumbs. Leave to cool. Add 1 beaten egg only if necessary to bind together. Mix ham, remaining breadcrumbs, garlic, sherry, nutmeg and seasonings. Beat in up to 2 of the eggs, 1 at a time, until mixture holds together. Put half the ham mixture into a 1lb glass loaf dish and pack down firmly. Make a channel down the center and mound the mushroom mixture into it. Cover with remaining ham mixture, packing it carefully around the mushroom mixture to cover it completely. Cover dish with plastic wrap and put into the microwave oven with a custard cup of water. Cook for 10 minutes on MEDIUM, leave to stand for 2 minutes, then cook for another 2 minutes on MEDIUM until firm. Cover with foil and weight the top of the dish. Chill for 4-5 hours and cut into slices to serve with toast or French bread.

Stuffed Tomatoes Provençal

PREPARATION TIME: 10 minutes

MICROWAVE COOKING TIME: 6 minutes

SERVES: 4 people

4 large ripe tomatoes
8oz mushrooms, finely chopped
1 shallot, finely chopped
2 tbsps butter or margarine
1 cup fresh white breadcrumbs
1 tbsp white wine
1 clove garlic, crushed
1 tsp Dijon mustard
1 tsp chopped parsley
1 tsp chopped basil
¼ tsp thyme

GARNISH
Parsley sprigs

Cut the rounded ends of the tomatoes off to form caps, and remove the green cores from the bottoms. Scoop out the pulp and seeds, and strain the juice. Put the butter into a small bowl with the garlic and shallot and cook for 2 minutes on HIGH. Stir in the mushrooms and wine and cook for 2 minutes on HIGH. Add breadcrumbs, herbs, seasoning, mustard and tomato pulp, and mix well. Stuff the tomatoes and put into a shallow

dish. Place the tops on at a slight angle and cook, uncovered, for 2 minutes on HIGH. Garnish with the parsley sprigs.

Langoustine Parisienne

PREPARATION TIME: 10 minutes

MICROWAVE COOKING TIME: 14 minutes

SERVES: 4 people

1lb langoustines, shelled and uncooked (Gulf shrimp may be substituted)
8oz mushrooms
⅔ cup butter or margarine
3 tbsps flour
1 shallot, finely chopped
1½ cups milk
1 tbsp chopped parsley
2 tbsps dry sherry
⅓ cup dry breadcrumbs
Lemon juice
Paprika
Salt
Pepper

Cut mushroom stalks level with the caps and cut mushrooms into quarters. Put 3 tbsps of the butter into a large bowl, then add shallot and cook for 1 minute on HIGH. Stir in the mushrooms and cook, uncovered, for 6 minutes on HIGH. Add flour and seasoning, and stir in the milk and sherry. Cook for 3 minutes on HIGH, stirring frequently. Add parsley, and set aside. Put langoustines into a small bowl with 2 tbsps water, cover with pierced plastic wrap and cook for 2 minutes on HIGH. Cut each langoustine into 2 or 3 pieces if large, then stir them into the mushroom sauce. Heat a browning tray and melt the remaining butter. Stir in the breadcrumbs and cook until golden brown and crisp. Put the shellfish-mushroom mixture into 4 custard cups and scatter over the crumbs. Sprinkle over the paprika and heat for 2 minutes on HIGH. If using a microwave convection oven, melt the butter for 1 minute on HIGH microwave setting, mix in the crumbs, fill the custard cups with the

shellfish-mushroom mixture and scatter the crumbs over. Sprinkle with paprika and cook for 3 minutes on the Combination setting to brown.

Chicken Liver Pâté

PREPARATION TIME: 8 minutes

MICROWAVE COOKING TIME: 9 minutes

SERVES: 4 people

1lb chicken livers
1 shallot, finely chopped
1 clove garlic, crushed
1 large sprig rosemary
1 tsp parsley
1 tbsp Madeira
1 tbsp cream
⅓ cup butter
Nutmeg
Salt
Pepper

GARNISH
Juniper berries
Small sprigs of rosemary

Pick over the livers, removing any discolored parts. Put livers, shallot, garlic, 1 sprig rosemary, half the butter, seasonings and a pinch of nutmeg into a bowl. Cover with pierced plastic wrap and cook for 6 minutes on HIGH, stirring once. Remove rosemary and put the mixture into a food processor with the Madeira, cream and parsley, and purée until smooth. Divide between 4 custard cups. Put remaining butter in a bowl and cook for 3 minutes on HIGH until boiling. Leave to stand and skim off salt rising to surface. Spoon the butter oil over each pâté to seal. Chill until firm, decorate with small sprigs of rosemary and juniper berries, and serve with hot toast or French bread.

Facing page: Chicken Liver Pâté (top) and Langoustine Parisienne (bottom).

Microwave

SOUPS AND APPETIZERS

MEAT AND SEAFOOD APPETIZERS

Sparkling Shrimp

PREPARATION TIME: 5 minutes

MICROWAVE COOKING TIME:
2½ minutes

SERVES: 4 people

1½ lbs peeled shrimp
1 tbsp peppercorns packed in brine, rinsed
½ cup dry sparkling white wine
½ cup heavy cream
Juice and grated rind of half an orange
Salt
Pepper

GARNISH
12 thin orange slices

Put orange rind and juice, peppercorns, seasoning and wine into a
bowl. Heat for 30 seconds on HIGH.
Stir in the shrimp and heat for
1 minute on HIGH. Lightly whip the
cream, fold in, and heat for a further
1 minute on HIGH. Adjust seasoning
before putting into serving dishes.
Garnish with the orange slices.

Moûles Marinière à la Moutarde

PREPARATION TIME: 5 minutes

MICROWAVE COOKING TIME:
9 minutes

SERVES: 4 people

2 pints mussels
1½ tbsps butter or margarine
2 shallots, finely chopped
1 clove garlic, crushed
4 tbsps Dijon mustard
1 cup white wine

½ cup heavy cream
1 tbsp flour
1 tbsp parsley, chopped
1 tbsp dill, chopped
Salt
Pepper

Scrub mussels well and discard any
that are open or broken. Put butter

**This page: Moûles Marinière à la
Moutarde.**
Facing page: Sparkling Shrimp.

into a large bowl and cook for
1 minute on HIGH. Add shallot,
garlic, wine and seasoning. Cover

with pierced plastic wrap and cook for 2 minutes on HIGH. Add mussels, and cover and cook for 3 minutes or until the shells are open. Stir half-way through the cooking time. Remove mussels from the bowl, put into a serving dish and keep them warm. Strain the liquid from them and set it aside. Put flour into a clean bowl and gradually pour on the mussel liquid, stirring well to mix. Cook, uncovered, for 2 minutes on HIGH or until thick, stirring occasionally. Stir in the mustard, cream and chopped herbs and heat through for 1 minute on HIGH. Pour over the mussels and serve with French bread.

Pork Satay with Peanut Sauce

PREPARATION TIME: 10 minutes and 1 hour to marinate pork

MICROWAVE COOKING TIME: 13 minutes

SERVES: 4 people

1½ lbs pork tenderloin, cut into 1″ cubes
1 large red pepper, cut into 1″ slices
2 tbsps oil
Lime juice
1 clove garlic, crushed
1 small green chili pepper, finely chopped
½ cup crunchy peanut butter
½ cup chicken or vegetable stock
1 tsp ground cumin
1 tsp ground coriander
1 shallot, finely chopped
Salt
Pepper

GARNISH
1 bunch fresh coriander leaves (optional)
Lemon wedges

Mix lime juice, salt and pepper together and mix in the pork. Leave in a cool place for 1 hour. Heat 1 tbsp oil in a small bowl and add shallot. Cook for 2 minutes on HIGH, add chili pepper and cook for 1 minute more on HIGH. Stir in stock, peanut butter, spices and seasoning. Cook for 1 minute on HIGH. Set aside.

Thread meat and red pepper onto 12 small, wooden skewers. Heat a browning tray for 5 minutes on HIGH. Add oil and brown the satay for 3 minutes on HIGH, turning frequently. Transfer onto a roasting rack, and cook for 6 minutes on MEDIUM. Arrange sprigs of coriander leaves on serving plates and put the satay on top. Spoon over some of the peanut sauce and serve the rest separately.

Spicy Chicken Kebabs with Avocado Sauce

PREPARATION TIME: 10 minutes

MICROWAVE COOKING TIME: 6 minutes

SERVES: 4 people

CHICKEN AND MARINADE
3 chicken breasts, skinned and boned
2 tbsps vegetable oil
1 clove garlic, crushed
1 tbsp curry powder

This page: Pork Satay with Peanut Sauce (top) and Spicy Chicken Kebabs with Avocado Sauce (bottom).
Facing page: Stuffed Zucchini.

¼ tsp Cayenne pepper
1 tbsp chopped coriander leaves
Juice and grated rind of 1 lime
Salt
Pepper

SAUCE
1 large avocado, peeled and stone removed
½ cup plain yogurt
1 tbsp vegetable oil
½ tsp finely chopped onion
1 tsp mango chutney
Lime juice

Cut chicken into strips 1″ wide. Combine ingredients for the marinade and mix in the chicken to coat each piece. Leave to marinate for 1 hour. Thread the meat onto wooden skewers and put onto a roasting rack. Cook for 5 minutes on

HIGH. Turn kebabs while cooking. Leave to stand, covered in plastic wrap, for 1 minute. Put oil and onion for the sauce into a small bowl. Cook for 1 minute on HIGH, and stir in chutney. Put avocado flesh into a food processor with seasoning, yogurt and lime juice. Add onion and chutney, and process until smooth. Serve with the chicken kebabs.

Stuffed Zucchini

PREPARATION TIME: 10 minutes

MICROWAVE COOKING TIME: 18 minutes

SERVES: 4 people

4 small, even-sized zucchini
¼lb crabmeat, fresh or frozen
1 shallot, finely chopped
½ cup cream cheese
½ cup mushrooms, chopped
¼ tsp tomato paste
¼ cup grated Parmesan cheese
4 tbsps dry breadcrumbs
2 tbsps milk
1 tbsp chopped parsley
4 tbsps butter, melted
Tabasco
Salt and pepper

Top and tail the zucchini and put into a large dish with 1 cup of water. Cover with pierced plastic wrap and cook for 4-5 minutes on HIGH. Rinse in cold water until completely cooled. Cut in half lengthwise, and carefully scoop out the flesh with a teaspoon, leaving a thin lining of flesh inside the skin. Leave to drain. Chop flesh roughly and set aside. Melt 2 tbsps of butter in a bowl for 1 minute on HIGH. Add the shallot and mushrooms, and cook, covered, for 2 minutes on HIGH. Add zucchini flesh, cover and cook for 1 minute on HIGH. Beat the cream cheese, tomato paste and milk together. Add crabmeat, parsley, seasoning, and a few drops of tabasco. Stir into the zucchini mixture and pile the filling into each zucchini shell. Mix breadcrumbs and Parmesan cheese together, and top each filled zucchini. Melt the remain-

ing butter and sprinkle over the zucchini. Heat through, uncovered, for 5 minutes on HIGH and brown under a broiler or on the Combination setting of a microwave convection oven for 10 minutes. Serve immediately.

Potted Smoked Fish

PREPARATION TIME: 15 minutes

MICROWAVE COOKING TIME: 8 minutes

SERVES: 4 people

2 smoked fish fillets
1 tbsp butter or margarine
1 tbsp flour
⅓ cup cream cheese
⅓ cup milk
6-8 pimento-stuffed olives, sliced
2 tsps Dijon mustard
Salt and pepper

GARNISH
½ cup butter for clarifying
Pimento-stuffed olives
Black peppercorns

Skin the fish fillets and break up into small pieces. Melt butter for 1 minute on HIGH. Stir in the flour and cook for 2 minutes on HIGH. Blend in the cheese, milk, half the olives, mustard and seasoning. Add fish and mix until well blended. Put into 4 custard cups and smooth the top. Cover each with plastic wrap and cook for 1 minute on HIGH to set the mixture. Put butter into a medium bowl and heat for 3-4 minutes on HIGH, or until boiling. Leave to stand for 10-15 minutes. Skim the salt off the top and spoon the butter oil carefully over each pot of fish. Fill nearly to the top, and leave until almost set. Then place the remaining olives and peppercorns on top of the butter. Chill and when set, cover the decoration with another thin layer of clarified butter and refrigerate again until set. Serve with hot toast.

Artichokes with Mustard Butter

PREPARATION TIME: 8 minutes

MICROWAVE COOKING TIME: 21 minutes

SERVES: 4 people

4 globe artichokes
1 tbsp lemon juice
Pinch salt
2 cups water
1 tbsp oil
1 bay leaf
1 slice onion

SAUCE
½ cup butter
3 tbsps Dijon mustard
Salt and pepper
Squeeze of lemon juice

Break stems from the base of each artichoke and twist to remove any stringy fibers. Trim the base of each so the artichokes sit level. Trim tips of artichoke leaves using kitchen scissors. Wash artichokes under cold running water. Put lemon juice, salt, water, oil, bay leaf and onion slice into a large bowl and cook 3-4 minutes on HIGH, or until the water boils. Put artichokes upright in the bowl, cover with plastic wrap and pierce several times. Cook for 15 minutes on HIGH, or until lower leaves can be pulled away easily. Leave to stand covered while preparing the sauce. Put butter, seasoning and lemon juice into a glass measuring cup or jug and cook for 2 minutes on HIGH, or until butter has melted. Beat in the mustard until sauce holds together. Put artichokes onto special artichoke serving plates, or onto small serving plates each on top of a larger plate, to give room for the discarded leaves. Serve the sauce separately, or remove the "choke" and serve the sauce in the center of the artichoke.

Facing page: Potted Smoked Fish (top) and Artichokes with Mustard Butter (bottom).

Microwave

SOUPS AND APPETIZERS

CHEESE AND EGG APPETIZERS

Eggs Florentine

PREPARATION TIME: 15 minutes

MICROWAVE COOKING TIME: 18 minutes

SERVES: 4 people

2¼ lbs fresh spinach, washed and stems removed
2 tbsps butter or margarine
4 eggs
2 tomatoes, skinned and seeded
Nutmeg
Salt
Pepper

MORNAY SAUCE
3 tbsps butter or margarine
3 tbsps flour
1½ cups milk
⅓ cup Cheddar cheese, grated
Dry mustard
Cayenne pepper
Salt
Pepper

To prepare spinach and tomatoes: Put spinach into a roasting bag and tie loosely. Stand upright and cook for 5 minutes on HIGH. (Spinach may also be cooked in a bowl covered with pierced plastic wrap.) Drain spinach well, and chop roughly. Boil 2 cups of water in a large bowl on HIGH and put in the tomatoes for 5 seconds. Put the tomatoes immediately into cold water. Peel, squeeze out the seeds and juice, and chop roughly. To poach the eggs: Pour water into each of 4 custard cups to a depth of 1". Put the dishes in a circle and heat on HIGH until the water boils. Break 1 egg into each cup and pierce the yoke with a sharp knife. Cook on DEFROST or LOW for 3 minutes,

or until whites have set. Turn the dishes at 1 minute intervals. To prepare Mornay sauce: Melt butter in a medium bowl for 1 minute on HIGH. Stir in the flour, mustard and a pinch of Cayenne pepper, and add the milk gradually. Cook for 4-5 minutes on HIGH, stirring frequently. Add the cheese, reserving some for the top. Add seasoning and stir until blended. Melt 2 tbsps of butter for 1 minute on HIGH. Stir in the spinach, seasoning and grated nutmeg to taste. Heat for 1 minute on HIGH, then add tomatoes. Put some of the spinach mixture into each individual serving dish and top with a poached egg. Coat each with Mornay sauce and sprinkle on grated cheese. Brown under a broiler, or on the Combination setting in a microwave convection oven for 2 minutes.

Baked Eggs with Mushrooms and Mustard Cream

PREPARATION TIME: 10 minutes

MICROWAVE COOKING TIME: 9 minutes

SERVES: 4 people

8oz mushrooms, finely chopped
4 eggs
½ cup cream, whipped
1oz chopped chives
1 tsp sherry
2 tsps Dijon mustard
Paprika
Salt
Pepper

Melt butter in a small bowl for 1 minute on HIGH. Add mushrooms and cook for 4 minutes on HIGH. Add chives, sherry and seasoning and divide into 4 custard cups. Make a slight well in the center of each portion and break an egg into it. Pierce the yoke with a small, sharp knife. Fold the mustard, cream and seasonings together and spoon over the eggs. Sprinkle with paprika and cook for 4 minutes on HIGH. Leave to stand for 1 minute before serving.

Cheese Custards

PREPARATION TIME: 10 minutes

MICROWAVE COOKING TIME: 30 minutes

SERVES: 4 people

¼ cup butter or margarine
¼ cup flour
½ tsp dry mustard
1 cup light cream
½ cup heavy cream
¾ cup Cheddar cheese, grated
4 eggs, separated
¼ tsp cream of tartar
Cayenne pepper
Salt
Pepper
Paprika

Melt the butter for 1 minute on HIGH. Add the flour, mustard, Cayenne pepper and seasoning to the bowl and stir in the cream gradually.

Facing page: Eggs Florentine (top) and Cheese Custards (bottom).

Cook for 6 minutes on HIGH, stirring frequently until thickened. Add ½ cup of the cheese and stir to melt. Beat in the egg yolks and beat egg whites with the cream of tartar until stiff but not dry. Fold whites into cheese mixture and pour into 8 small custard cups. Arrange in a larger dish filled with hot water. Cook for 3 minutes on HIGH. Turn the cups and cook for 1½ minutes more on HIGH. If the mixture appears set and begins to pull away from the sides of the cups, turn the custards out. If not, cook for 30 seconds longer on HIGH. Put the custards into individual baking dishes, allowing 2 per person. Pour over the heavy cream and sprinkle on the remaining cheese and paprika. Bake for 2 minutes on HIGH and serve immediately.

Sour Cream and Caviar Cheesecake

PREPARATION TIME: 10 minutes

MICROWAVE COOKING TIME: 15 minutes

SERVES: 4 people

1 cup Cheddar cheese crackers
¼ cup butter
2 tbsps Parmesan cheese
8oz package cream cheese
1 cup Gruyère cheese, grated
¼ cup milk
2 eggs
½ cup sour cream
⅓ cup chives, chopped
1 jar red salmon caviar
1 jar black lumpfish caviar

Crush the crackers in a food processor and melt the butter for 1 minute on HIGH. Add half the Parmesan cheese and all the butter to the crumbs in the processor and work until well mixed. Mix cream cheese, Gruyère and remaining Parmesan together. Beat in eggs and sour cream, reserving 2 tbsps for the top, and stir in the chives. Add seasoning. Line the base of a 6" microwave cake pan with wax paper

and pour in the cheesecake mixture. Bake for 5 minutes on HIGH until lightly set. Sprinkle on the crumbs and press down gently. Bake for another 10 minutes on MEDIUM. Leave to cool at room temperature, then chill for 1 hour. Invert onto a serving dish, spread with remaining sour cream and decorate the top with caviar. Cut into wedges to serve.

Eggplant Caviar

PREPARATION TIME: 30 minutes

MICROWAVE COOKING TIME: 13 minutes

SERVES: 4 people

This page: Sour Cream and Caviar Cheesecake.
Facing page: Baked Eggs with Mushrooms and Mustard Cream (top) and Eggplant Caviar (bottom).

1 large or 2 small eggplants
1 clove garlic, crushed
4 tbsps olive oil
Juice of half a lemon
2 tsps chopped fresh coriander
1 tbsp chopped parsley
1 tsp cumin seeds
1 cap pimento, finely chopped
Cayenne pepper
Salt
Pepper
Pitta bread

Dice the eggplant, then spread out on paper towels, sprinkle with salt

and leave for 30 minutes to draw out any bitterness. Rinse and dry well. Put into a large bowl with 4 tbsps water, cover with pierced plastic wrap and cook for 10 minutes on HIGH, stirring 2-3 times. Drain and leave to cool. Put cumin seeds on a plate and roast, uncovered, for 3 minutes on HIGH, stirring occasionally. Put the eggplant into a food processor with the garlic, and blend until smooth, adding olive oil slowly through the feed tube. Add lemon juice, seasoning, Cayenne pepper and cumin seeds, and process once. Add herbs and pimento and process again once. Adjust seasoning and chill. Wrap pitta bread in paper towels and warm for 30 seconds on HIGH. Cut into triangles and serve with the eggplant caviar.

Pasta Shells Stuffed with Garlic Cheese

PREPARATION TIME: 10 minutes

MICROWAVE COOKING TIME: 20 minutes

SERVES: 4 people

8 large pasta shells (conchiglie)
2 pkts garlic and herb soft cheese
4 tomatoes, skinned and seeded
3 tbsps butter or margarine
3 tbsps flour
2 cups milk
½ cup Gruyère cheese, grated
1 tbsp chopped parsley
Nutmeg
Salt and pepper

Heat 4 cups water on HIGH for 5 minutes, until boiling. Put in the tomatoes for 5 seconds, then remove them and put immediately into cold water. Peel, seed and shred them thinly, then set aside. Put the pasta into the water with 1 tbsp oil and cook for 9 minutes, or until just tender. Leave to stand for 5 minutes. Drain and dry. Beat cheese to soften. Put into a pastry bag fitted with a wide, plain tube. Fill each shell with the garlic cheese and put into 4 baking dishes. Melt butter in a

small bowl for 1 minute on HIGH and stir in the flour. Stir in the milk and seasoning, and blend well. Heat for 2-3 minutes on HIGH, stirring frequently. Add half of the cheese, stirring to melt. Stir in the tomato strips and coat over the pasta shells in the baking dishes. Sprinkle on the remaining cheese. Heat for 2 minutes on HIGH. Serve immediately.

This page: Pasta Shells Stuffed with Garlic Cheese.
Facing page: Stuffed Vine Leaves Bordelaise.

VEGETABLE APPETIZERS

Stuffed Vine Leaves Bordelaise

PREPARATION TIME: 15 minutes

MICROWAVE COOKING TIME:
53 minutes and 5 minutes standing
time

SERVES: 4 people

12 packaged vine leaves
¼ cup butter
1 shallot, finely chopped
1 cup mushrooms, finely chopped
½ cup rice
4 strips bacon (rind and bones removed)
2 tbsps dried blackcurrants
1 tbsp parsley
Salt and pepper

SAUCE
1 shallot, finely chopped
1½ tbsps flour
1½ tbsps butter or margarine
¾ cup red wine
¾ cup beef stock
1 clove garlic, crushed
1 tsp tomato paste

To make stuffed vine leaves: Put
3 cups water and the rice into a large,
deep bowl. Cover with pierced
plastic wrap and cook for 14 minutes
on HIGH. Add the blackcurrants and
leave to stand for 5 minutes. Drain
and cool. Put the butter and shallot
for the filling into a bowl, cover and
cook for 1 minute on HIGH. Add
mushrooms and cook for 6 minutes
on HIGH, stirring occasionally. Heat
a browning dish for 3-4 minutes on
HIGH and cook the bacon for
1 minute each side until crisp.
Crumble the bacon and add to the
mushrooms with the rice, parsley and
seasoning. Mix well and put a mound

of filling on each leaf. Roll up, tucking in the sides to enclose the filling completely.

To make the sauce: Heat a browning dish for 3-4 minutes on HIGH. Melt the butter and add shallot and flour. Cook until golden brown, or about 4 minutes on HIGH. Put into a bowl and stir in the stock, wine, garlic, tomato paste and seasoning. Cook, covered with pierced plastic wrap, for 4 minutes on HIGH. Put vine leaves into a casserole, seamed side down, and pour over the sauce. Cover and cook for 5 minutes on HIGH. Serve immediately.

Celeriac Moutarde

PREPARATION TIME: 10 minutes

MICROWAVE COOKING TIME: 15 minutes

SERVES: 4 people

1 large root celeriac, peeled
2 tbsps white wine

MUSTARD CREAM SAUCE
3 tbsps butter
3 tbsps flour
2 cups milk
4 tbsps Dijon mustard
1 tbsp celery seed
Salt and pepper
4 tbsps dry breadcrumbs
2 tbsps butter or margarine

Cut celeriac into ¼″ slices, then into sticks about 1″ long. Put into a bowl with the wine, and toss to mix. Cover with pierced plastic wrap and cook for 4 minutes on HIGH. Melt butter in a small deep bowl for 1 minute on HIGH. Add flour and cook for 1 minute more on HIGH. Stir in milk, mustard, celery seed and strained cooking liquid from the celeriac. Season and cook for 3 minutes on HIGH, stirring occasionally, until sauce has thickened. Put celeriac into 4 baking dishes and coat with the sauce. Heat a browning tray for 3-4 minutes on HIGH. Put in 2 tbsps butter and dry breadcrumbs, and cook until golden brown. Sprinkle the breadcrumbs on

top of the celeriac and heat through for 2 minutes on HIGH. If using a microwave convection oven, melt the butter for 1 minute, then stir in the breadcrumbs. Sprinkle on top of the celeriac and cook on the Combination setting for 5 minutes. Serve immediately.

Vinaigrette de Jardin

PREPARATION TIME: 15 minutes

MICROWAVE COOKING TIME: 7 minutes

SERVES: 4 people

SALAD AND DRESSING
4oz pea pods
2 zucchini, sliced in rounds
4 green onions, sliced
4oz broccoli flowerets
1 small head cauliflower, cut into flowerets
2 carrots, sliced in rounds
4 tomatoes, seeded and sliced into strips
1 banana pepper, sliced into strips
6 tbsps olive oil
2 tbsps white wine vinegar
1 tbsp Dijon mustard
1 tbsp herbs (eg chives, chervil, parsley, basil), chopped
Salt and pepper

GARLIC BREAD
1 small loaf French bread
⅓ cup butter
1 clove garlic, crushed
2 tbsps poppy seeds

Cook each of the vegetables on HIGH in 2 tbsps water, in a shallow, covered dish: pea pods, 2 minutes; zucchini, 3 minutes; broccoli, 3 minutes; cauliflower, 5 minutes; carrots, 5 minutes. When cooked, rinse immediately in cold water to stop the cooking. Drain and leave to dry. Boil 2 cups water for 3-4 minutes on HIGH and put tomatoes in for 5 seconds. Then put them immediately into cold water, peel and quarter them, remove the seeds, and cut them into thin shreds. Cut pepper into thin slices and add, with the tomato, to the drained vegetables. Mix oil, vinegar, Dijon

mustard, herbs and seasoning, and pour over the mixed vegetables. Toss lightly and leave to marinate. Serve with the garlic bread.

To make garlic bread: Cut the loaf into thick slices without cutting through the base. Mix the butter, garlic and poppy seed, and spread between each slice. Wrap loosely in paper towels and heat for 1½ minutes on HIGH or until butter has melted. Serve with the vegetable salad.

Cheese and Herb Soufflés

PREPARATION TIME: 8 minutes

MICROWAVE COOKING TIME: 8-10 minutes

SERVES: 4 people

1 cup Colby and Parmesan cheese, grated and mixed
¼ cup butter or margarine
¼ cup flour
1½ cups milk
6 eggs, separated
1 tsp cream of tartar
¼ tsp parsley, chopped
¼ tsp chives, chopped
¼ tsp thyme, chopped
¼ tsp sage, chopped
Dry mustard
Paprika
Salt
Pepper

Put the butter in a bowl and heat for 1 minute on HIGH. Stir in the flour, Cayenne pepper and mustard, and blend in the milk. Cook for 4 minutes on HIGH, stirring frequently until thickened. Add cheese, herbs and seasoning. Beat egg yolks into the cheese mixture one at a time. Beat egg whites until stiff but not dry with the cream of tartar, and fold in carefully. Divide the mixture between 4 small soufflé dishes. Cook on MEDIUM for 4-6 minutes. The

Facing page: Cheese and Herb Soufflés (top) and Celeriac Moutarde (bottom).

inside the shell. Sprinkle the scooped-out flesh and shell with lemon juice. Heat a browning tray for 3 minutes on HIGH, brown bacon for 1 minute each side, crumble it and set aside. Brown shallot, pepper and mushrooms lightly for 1 minute in the bacon fat and combine with avocado flesh. Melt 1 tbsp butter for 1 minute on HIGH. Stir in flour and milk. Heat for 2 minutes until thickened, stirring frequently. Add all ingredients save cheese and breadcrumbs. Stir in seasoning and a few drops of tabasco. Pile into the shells. Sprinkle on the cheese and breadcrumbs. Melt remaining butter for 1 minute. Sprinkle over the avocado and cook for 3 minutes in a microwave-convection oven on Combination setting, or brown under a broiler. Serve immediately.

Stuffed Mushrooms

PREPARATION TIME: 8 minutes

MICROWAVE COOKING TIME: 6-8 minutes

SERVES: 4 people

12-16 large mushrooms
4oz ham, finely chopped
½ cup fresh white breadcrumbs
⅓ cup finely chopped walnuts
1 egg, beaten
1 bunch snipped chives
1 tbsp chopped parsley
1 tbsp Dijon mustard
Dry breadcrumbs
3 tbsps butter, melted
Salt
Pepper

Clean the mushrooms, trimming stalks, and chop them finely. Mix with the ham, breadcrumbs, walnuts, herbs, mustard and seasoning. Beat in the egg gradually to bind. Pile on top of the mushrooms, then put on a

COMBINATION setting of a microwave convection oven may be used for 6 minutes. Sprinkle with paprika and serve immediately.

Stuffed Avocados

PREPARATION TIME: 10 minutes

MICROWAVE COOKING TIME: 10 minutes

SERVES: 4 people

2 large avocados
4 slices smoked bacon

1 cup peeled cooked shrimp, shelled
1 shallot, finely chopped
½ cup mushrooms, roughly chopped
1 green pepper, roughly chopped
1½ tbsps butter or margarine
2 tbsps flour
½ cup milk
2 tomatoes, skinned, seeded and chopped
⅓ cup Parmesan cheese
4 tbsps dry breadcrumbs
1 tbsp parsley
1 tsp marjoram
Tabasco
Salt and pepper
Lemon juice

Halve avocados and remove stones. Scoop out flesh, leaving ¼" lining

**This page: Vinaigrette de Jardin.
Facing page: Stuffed Avocados (top) and Stuffed Mushrooms (bottom).**

plate and cook for 5 minutes on
HIGH. Sprinkle over the dry crumbs
and melted butter. Cook for a further
1 minute on HIGH. Brown under a
broiler, or cook for 2 minutes in a
microwave-convection oven on the
Combination setting.

Spinach Gnocchi in Ricotta Sauce

PREPARATION TIME: 10 minutes

MICROWAVE COOKING TIME:
8 minutes

SERVES: 4 people

GNOCCHI
1lb fresh spinach, washed and stems
  removed
1 cup Gruyère cheese, grated
4 slices white bread, crusts removed
2 tbsps finely chopped walnuts
1 tbsp finely chopped shallot
1 clove garlic, crushed
1 egg, beaten
Nutmeg
Salt
Pepper

RICOTTA SAUCE
8oz Ricotta cheese
3 tbsps grated Parmesan cheese
½ tsp basil, fresh or dried
¼ tsp chopped parsley
⅔ cup cream or milk
Salt
Pepper
Paprika

To prepare gnocchi: Put spinach into
a roasting bag and tie loosely. Stand
upright and cook for 3 minutes on
HIGH. (Spinach may also be cooked
in a bowl covered with pierced
plastic wrap.) Drain the spinach well,
and chop finely. Make crumbs from
the bread slices using a food
processor or liquidizer. Add to the
spinach along with the Gruyère,
walnuts, nutmeg, seasoning and egg.
Beat well and shape into 2″ balls or
ovals. Put gnocchi onto a plate, cover
loosely with plastic wrap, and cook
for 2 minutes on HIGH. Set aside
and keep warm.
To make sauce: Mix Ricotta cheese
with the other ingredients except the

paprika and heat for 1 minute on
HIGH.
Divide the gnocchi between 4 gratin
dishes and coat with the sauce.
Sprinkle with paprika and heat for
2 minutes on HIGH. Serve at once.

Salade Alsacienne

PREPARATION TIME: 10 minutes

MICROWAVE COOKING TIME:
13-15 minutes

SERVES: 4 people

¾ lb new potatoes, scrubbed but not
  peeled (or regular potatoes, peeled)
Half head (white) cabbage, shredded
2 tbsps white wine
8oz smoked sausage or kielbasa

2 tsps caraway seeds
½ cup blue cheese, crumbled
½ cup sour cream
1 tbsp white wine vinegar
3 tbsps vegetable oil
¼ tsp French mustard
Salt
Pepper

GARNISH
4 green onions, chopped

Prick potato skins with a fork, if using
new potatoes. Put potatoes into a
casserole dish with 2 tbsps water,
cover, and cook for 10-12 minutes on
HIGH until tender. Drain and cut
into large pieces. Mix vinegar, oil,
mustard and seasoning together and
pour over the potatoes. Stir and
leave to stand. Prick sausage skin and
cook, covered, for 1 minute on

HIGH. Slice thinly and add to the potatoes. Put cabbage into a casserole dish with the wine, caraway seeds and seasoning. Cover and cook for 2 minutes on HIGH. Add to the potatoes and sausages. Add blue cheese and sour cream, and mix carefully, so that the potatoes do not break up. Garnish with chopped green onions.

Fondue Pots

PREPARATION TIME: 10 minutes
MICROWAVE COOKING TIME: 10-13 minutes
SERVES: 4 people

FONDUE
2 cups Gruyère cheese, grated

Facing page: Spinach Gnocchi in Ricotta Sauce.
This page: Salade Alsacienne (left) and Fondue Pots (right).

2 cups Swiss cheese, grated
1½ cups dry white wine
1½ tbsps cornstarch
1½ tbsps kirsch
1 clove garlic, crushed
Dry mustard
Nutmeg
Salt and Pepper

BREADSTICKS
12 slices white bread, crusts removed
1 stick butter
4 tbsps herbs (eg thyme, parsley, sage) chopped

To make breadsticks: Roll out each slice of bread to flatten. Mix herbs and half the butter together and spread over the bread. Roll up from each end to the middle and cut in half to form 2 breadsticks. Melt remaining butter for 1 minute on HIGH and brush over breadsticks. Put bread onto a plate and cook for 5 minutes in a microwave convection oven on the Combination setting until pale brown. Keep warm. (Breadsticks may also be baked in a conventional oven for 20 minutes at 400°F, 200°C.)
To make fondue: Put garlic, wine, mustard, nutmeg and seasoning into a bowl and cook for 5 minutes on HIGH. Mix cornstarch, kirsch and cheese, and blend well into the wine. Cook for 5-8 minutes on MEDIUM, stirring frequently until thick and

creamy. Heat individual custard cups and pour fondue mixture into each. Serve immediately with the warm breadsticks or raw vegetables.

Garlic Mushrooms

PREPARATION TIME: 5 minutes

MICROWAVE COOKING TIME: 6 minutes

SERVES: 4 people

1½ lbs mushrooms, cleaned and quartered
2 cloves garlic, crushed
¼ cup butter
3 tbsps white wine
8 slices French bread, ½″ thick
¼ tsp fresh thyme, chopped
¼ tsp fresh sage, chopped
¼ tsp parsley, chopped
Salt
Pepper

GARNISH
2 tbsps chopped chives

Heat butter for 1 minute on HIGH or until melted in a large bowl. Add garlic and cook for 2 minutes on HIGH. Mix in the herbs, wine, seasoning and mushrooms. Pour into a shallow casserole, and cook, uncovered, for 3 minutes on HIGH. Heat the bread for 1 minute on HIGH. Garnish with snipped chives and serve on French bread.

Leek and Ham Tarts Bernaise

PREPARATION TIME: 10 minutes

MICROWAVE COOKING TIME: 19½ minutes

SERVES: 4 people

TART SHELLS AND FILLING
8-12 slices wholewheat bread, crusts removed
1-2 leeks, washed and sliced
¼ cup butter or margarine
4oz ham, chopped
2½ tbsps flour
3 tbsps white wine
2 tbsps milk or chicken stock

BERNAISE SAUCE
½ cup butter
3 egg yolks
1 tbsp white wine or tarragon vinegar
1 bay leaf

**This page: Leek and Ham Tarts Bernaise (top) and Garlic Mushrooms (bottom).
Facing page: Pumpkin Creams with Dill Sauce.**

1 blade mace
1 tsp chopped tarragon
1 tsp chopped parsley
Salt
Pepper
Lemon juice

To prepare shells and filling: Roll out the slices of bread to flatten slightly. Cut out large rounds with a pastry cutter. Melt half the butter for 1 minute on HIGH and brush over both sides of the bread rounds. Mold into custard cups or a muffin pan and cook for 3 minutes on HIGH until crisp. Melt the remaining butter in a bowl for 1 minute on HIGH and add the leek slices. Cover with pierced plastic wrap and cook for 8 minutes on HIGH, stirring occasionally. Add ham and flour, and cook for 1 minute on HIGH. Stir in the wine, milk or stock, and seasoning. Cook, uncovered, for 2 minutes or until sauce thickens. Set aside.

To make Bernaise sauce: Have a bowl of ice water ready. Melt the butter in a deep bowl on HIGH for 1 minute. Put vinegar, bay leaf and mace in a small dish and heat through for 30 seconds on HIGH. Beat egg yolks and seasoning together and strain on the vinegar. Pour into the bowl with the butter and stir well. Cook for 15 seconds on HIGH, remove bowl and stir sauce. Repeat until sauce has thickened – which takes about 2 minutes. Put bowl immediately into ice water to stop the cooking. Remove the prepared shells from the custard cups and put onto a plate. Fill with the ham and leek mixture and coat each with a spoonful of the Bernaise sauce. Broil until lightly browned. Serve immediately.

Pumpkin Creams with Dill Sauce

PREPARATION TIME: 15 minutes

MICROWAVE COOKING TIME: 27 minutes

SERVES: 4 people

2½ cups mashed pumpkin
1 shallot, finely chopped
½ cup Ricotta cheese
½ cup Parmesan cheese, grated
2 eggs
¼ cup sour cream
¼ pint/½ cup heavy cream
1 tbsp parsley
2 bunches dill
Crushed garlic (optional)
Nutmeg
Salt
Pepper

GARNISH
Whole sprigs of dill

Put the mashed pumpkin into a food processor and add eggs, shallot, cheeses, parsley, nutmeg and seasoning. Process until well blended. Divide between 4 custard cups and cook for 6 minutes on HIGH until set. Leave to stand for 5 minutes before turning out. Heat the cream for 2 minutes on HIGH in a small bowl with the crushed garlic, if desired. Chop the dill finely, reserving 4 whole sprigs. Stir the chopped dill into the hot cream with the sour cream. Turn out the pumpkin creams and serve immediately with the dill sauce. Garnish with whole sprigs of dill.

INDEX